Bibliographic information published by the German National Library:

The German National Library lists this publication in the National Bibliography; detailed bibliographic data are available on the Internet at http://dnb.dnb.de .

Imprint:

Copyright © 2011 GRIN Verlag, Open Publishing GmbH
Print and binding: Books on Demand GmbH, Norderstedt Germany
ISBN: 978-3-668-18699-6

This book at GRIN:

http://www.grin.com/en/e-book/318146/basic-concepts-of-discrimination-at-work-a-literature-review

Vastal Shah

Basic Concepts of Discrimination at Work. A Literature Review

GRIN Publishing

GRIN - Your knowledge has value

Since its foundation in 1998, GRIN has specialized in publishing academic texts by students, college teachers and other academics as e-book and printed book. The website www.grin.com is an ideal platform for presenting term papers, final papers, scientific essays, dissertations and specialist books.

Visit us on the internet:

http://www.grin.com/

http://www.facebook.com/grincom

http://www.twitter.com/grin_com

Contents

1 Introduction

This text focuses on the historical and theoretical models of discrimination in a cultur-ally, racially, ethnically and nationally diverse workplace. This is achieved by reviewing a va-riety of academic books and renowned journal articles, getting a sound know-how of the theo-ries pertaining to discrimination, its role in different diverse workplaces, focusing on South Asia, especially Pakistan, and then studying them thoroughly by comparing and contrasting different case studies of countries globally. All great insights into the issues of the variables under scrutiny are connected and related with the overall theme of this study and thrown light upon elaborately.

2 Defining and Measuring Discrimination at Work

Before discussing the historical trends of employment discrimination and its effect on the modern world, it is important to define discrimination in general and in the context of a workplace and mark its perimeters accordingly: how it is measured and how it will affect this study. Businesses around the world are interested in recognizing the dire need to address the diversity and multicultural issues in workplace practices (Arredondo, 1996; Cox, 1993; Daly, 1998; Sue, 1995). Contrary to popular belief that diversity encourages tolerance and broad-mindedness in a work setting, there has been incidents recorded stating otherwise. (State refer-ence)

2.1 Discrimination and Equality at Workplaces: Defining the Concepts

There are several forms of discrimination throughout history. For this study, discrimi-nation will be discussed in the context of a diverse workplace. These include discrimination against an individual's race, gender, sexual orientation, disability and nationality. In the previ-ous literatures, several definitions of discrimination has emerged. According to Dipboye and Colella (2006, p.1 & 2) discrimination at workplace or employment discrimination is when employees are treated unfairly on the basis of their race, gender, nationality etc as compared to the majority or the host country national.

2.2 Measuring Discrimination at Workplace

Burkard et al. (2002) have described and critiqued five measures of workplace discrim-ination, prejudice, and diversity. These are as follows: the Workplace Prejudice/Discrimination Inventory (WPDI) (James, Lovato, & Cropanzano, 1994), the Attitudes Toward Diversity Scale

(ATDS) (Montei, Adams, & Eggers, 1996), the Organizational Diversity Inventory (ODI) (Hegarty & Dalton, 1995), the Workforce Diversity Questionnaire (WDQ) (Larkey, 1996), and the Perceived Occupational Opportunity Scale–Form B (POOS) and Perceived Occupational Discrimination Scale–Form B (PODS) (Chung & Harmon, 1999).

The Workplace Prejudice/Discrimination Inventory (WPDI) measures the employee's perceptions of prejudice and discrimination in their workplaces (James et al., 1994). It uses the 7-point Liket type scale that reflects the measure of prejudice and discrimination prevalent in the work environment.

The Attitudes Toward Diversity Scale (ATDS) was designed in order to scale the behavior of elements involved in their dealings with diversity. There are 10 components that make up these elements and they are categorized into three parts. These parts are made as elements in their association towards colleagues, bosses, and decisions related to promotions as well as human resource (Montei, Adams, & Eggers, 1996).

The Organizational Diversity Inventory (ODI) has 20 components divided into five categories: the presence of discrimination, discrimination with respect to a specific party, management of discrimination, management of people in small groups, and finally, mindset towards smaller groups (Hegarty & Dalton, 1995).

The Workforce Diversity Questionnaire (WDQ) was created with the goal of measuring relationships between diverse kinds of groups. It has scales that measure qualities such as acceptance, ideation, the ability to understand others, and the type of behavior that is shown (Larkey, 1996).

Lastly, the Perceived Occupational Opportunity Scale–Form B (POOS) and Perceived Occupational Discrimination Scale–Form B (PODS). It was created in order to explore the apparent professional chances given to Black Americans (Chung & Harmon, 1999).

3   Employment Discrimination: An International Historical Overview

Several scholars and researchers have studied the trends of the nature of discrimination and how it is important to strive for equality in the workplaces (Krieger, 1995; Reskin, 2000; Sturm, 1998, 2001). In United States of America, the Title VII of the Civil rights Act was formed in 1964 against the acts of discrimination in workplaces (Green, 2003). This was the time when multinationals started to appear in the business arena and globalized workforces, labour mobility increased, which resulted in the need to set more modern egalitarian rules in

3

the international work setting for flexible governance in the organization in order to enhance productivity.

Discrimination has been prevalent in the workplaces throughout the world since the dawn of time. In the previous era, the form of discrimination was clearly identifiable. It was prevalent in "social interaction, perception, evaluation and disbursement of opportunity" (Green, 2003, p.91). Keeping the World War II as a bench mark, looking at the pre-World War II era, there was strong racial discrimination against the Jews throughout Europe. They had different public place areas, they were exempted from certain public places. Natives Europeans casted them out socially and politically so they were forced to live in ghetto. While there was strong racial discrimination against black from whites, may it be South America or South Africa. South Africa was subject to the strongest form of racial discrimination as termed to be the Apartheid Era in their history. Such racial discrimination against the Black population, just like the Europeans Jews pre-world war II, they were also forced to live in the ghettos dues to social and political exclusion, while the basis of the Civil war in America was that North Americans were in favor of equal rights with the American Black population while people from South America strongly opposed it.

During the post-world war era, when women started to take active part in the workforce, the nature of their jobs mostly involved menial work with jobs such as secretary, nurses and so on. Their bosses were mostly men. This was the era when feminism was at its peak and women were striving to make a mark in the business world edge-by-edge despite the gender discrimination they had to face. Now, in the modern era, although minorities and women have managed to make a mark in the workforce successfully, "inequality in advancement and wages persists" (Green, 2003, p.96).

4 Theories on Discrimination at Workplace

Scholars have introduced theories to explain different discriminatory practices in workplaces throughout history.

4.1 Disparate Treatment Theory

Disparate Treatment Theory is one amongst two of the theories of discrimination in United States Civil Rights Act. Disparate Treatment Theory understands and views discrimination as specific, personal, possible to measure ad well as still, seeing the framework of the understanding of the respective person who makes judgement at the time. Disparate treatment doctrine needs as a condition that discrimination has to be intentional, that is to say, it should be possible to see a clear, awareness in discrimination of the event (Reeves v. Sanderson Plumbing Prod., Inc., 2000). It is this condition that led in the following years to the perception of discrimination as an act undertaken by a singular individual who has prejudices and discriminating beliefs in his mind against those that he discriminates against. In simple words, it can be understood by seeing that the disparate treatment theory is basically an investigation into the mind of the person who takes the decision in a case of discrimination. In order to understand the do justice to a victim affected by discrimination, the important thing was to consider what was the decision-maker's choice and mindset, understanding his biases and motivations for the particular act. Moreover, it was to be understood in relation to the particular time when the act took place.

It is possible to see this ideology and determiner of discrimination act by understanding the mind of the decision maker not only when the victim is an individual, but even when a group of people have made an allegation of being discriminated because of their personal characteristics.

With respect to the above mentioned determination approach, there are two methods in Disparate Treatment Theory: Indirect Method and Direct Method.

In direct method, the victim tries to prove that the reason for the reason for job-related decision was motivated by the fact that the victim was a part of a certain class. To support this, he offers evidence which is direct. For instance, the victim may try to show that the decision-maker had explicitly expressed that his decision was inspired by an intention to discriminate. However, direct evidence of such kind is usually never possible to have. This is simply because no employer is ready to admit such intention.

In such circumstances, it is possible for the victim to provide the following evidences:

He may try to provide evidence that there were certain comments and behaviors towards the group's other members by the decision-maker. This is based on statements that are either on paper or are oral. He may provide other information of this kind that may lead to the intent (Troupe v. May Department Stores, 1994). Other type of evidence is to show that employees of other groups, who were also in a similar situation, did not receive the same behavior and, in fact, were treated better (Marshall v. American Hospital Assoc., 1998). The other type of evidence that a victim may give is based on him not getting a job that he was qualified for, while another person not from his group got the job.

The other method is the indirect method. It is used in most cases since direct method is not possible to use as evidence is hard to find. In such situation, evidence of discrimination is proven by inference.

4.2 Spontaneous Discrimination

Spontaneous Discrimination theory believes that discrimination can emerge spontaneously. It may arise as a type of social habit irrespective of the racial framework of people or evidence of any such differences between two people. Usually, a person discriminates against another group in order to avoid such discrimination from one's own group. It is seen that before a person chooses to mingle with another person, he tries to understand the interactions that other person has had before, the groups these associations were made with. Conditioning, thus, emerges from the decisions made on the basis of such information.

It is found that there is a certain ratio of discrimination in specific situations. For instance, the first type is that people belonging to all races discriminate against those who have a different skin color. On the other hand, the other types of ratios feature discrimination only from one party. For instance, people of one race who show partial behavior towards other and those who are the victims try to be indifferent to color or just faintly discriminate.

In studies it has been found that discrimination as well as belonging to a group may really not be connected to traits related to payoff. People develop liking for their own groups members even when these groups were not natural but artificially made (Tajfel, 1970). In such studies, people show a lot of bias towards their own group.

In another experiment, it was seen that experience of discrimination as well as prejudice is possible to Design artificially and is possible to manipulate by changing the social environment (Sherif, 1961).

Viewpoints related to race change in accordance with the social environment (Minard, 1952).

In a study prong the spontaneous discrimination theory, the subject in the form of q white person was shown to discriminate against a black person solely because he was scared that if he chose not to discriminate, he would find it hard to get hired by other white people. Thus, a discriminative behavior is found to be in relationship to the fear of being punished by one's own group. We can compare this to how crossing a line in a specific group leads to isolation of that individual (Austen-Smith and Fryer, 2005).

Kandori (1992) talks about a situation in which members of two groups have been exposed to each other many times. After a certain amount of time, members from each group are selected randomly, and two such bad couples play a game. Each such players has been given a label that gives information about their actions in the past. It was found that those who played chose to change their behavior on the basis of labels, even though they had nothing much better to do with the results of the game. Taking actions on the basis of information not relevant to results is possible. Further, in some situations, stable ratios include discrimination (Peski and Szentes, 2012).

4.3 Other Theories

Phelps (1972) observed that the difference in the salary of black and white employees could be explained by seeing that the level of how productive a person is was seeing interrelated to that employee's color. This, color is seen as a symbol of productivity of an employee.

Arrow (1973) observed that discrimination was possibly a consequence of personal expectations. It was seen that the employees expected black employees to give less of their commitment than white employees to the work. Therefore, they were given less monetary results than white employees.

For an insight into statistical discrimination theory, one is advised to see Coate and Loury (1993), Moro and Norman (2004), Rosén (1997), Mailath, Samuelson, and Shaked (2000) and Lang, Manove, and Dickens (2005).

Gneezy, List, and Price (2012) did experiments on the group in many markets and used the characteristics of people in order to indenting the source of behavior related to discrimination. They found out that when it is perceived that the party that is discriminated is possible to control, then that discrimination is based on taste. If it is not, the. It is of statistical.

Mailath and Postlewaite (2006) presented a model in which men and women, after a certain time, were matched with each other and produced children. It was seen that people who had certain attributes (like blue eyes), were better in the behavior they were shown than those without it. Here, people with high endowment but without attributes preferred to match with low endowment people rather than high endowment people without attributes. This seen so because of the behavior of people to avoid risks- the behavior of people with high endowment shoed that tried to gather attributes for their offsprings. In simple words, they tried to transfer weather to the future generation through biological means.

5   Managing Diverse Workplace: Does it solve the Issue of Workplace Discrimination?

The concept of managing a diverse workplace is becoming more and more significant and getting recognition as an important concept to study and research (Konrad, 2003). Many scholars have developed various research papers to understand topics related to this. For instance, some scholars have presented findings on the ideas related to the problems of representation in discrimination (Darity & Mason, 1998; Hoque & Noon, 1999; Modood et al., 1998).

Others have discussed the validity of certain approaches and concepts of managers (Healy et al., 2004; Liff, 1999; Liff & Dickens, 1999).

These studies have done the work of making the topic element to policy-makers when it comes to equality. On the other hand, a number of concepts related to diversity have found a lot of research while others have not.

Research on the topic of diversity in the workplace has emerged and developed in different directions. If one wishes to categorize this, one can use three wide categories: research and studies on the appropriateness of a certain approach(related to managing diversity as well as producing equality), studies that explained the consequence of diversity on the outcomes of an organizations, and studies that explained the topics of discrimination in relation to some aspect of work.

A very important question in the topic of management in human resource is related to the validity of the method taken up by managers as well as scholars related to finding and pointing out issues in management of people. Scholars have differing approaches and view on getting equality in opportunity using liberal as well as radical methods in the 1980s (Jewson & Mason, 1986). On the other hand, some used the approaches of short as well as long-term strategies (Cockburn, 1989). By the 90s, however, the conversation has shifted to the topic of The appropriateness related to equal opportunity (Kandola and Fullerton, 1994). These scholars question whether the framework of equal opportunity was right. Their argument was based on the observation that equal opportunities were a part of a view that was based on groups. They further argued that this method was not appropriate while managing people's concerns as well as resolving the issues of modern organizations (Kessler & Purcell, 1995).

Now a very significant topic of this debate is the conversation on diversity and equality, focusing on finding ways for an organization to gain an environment where all people contribute with all their potential in order to make the business successful (Cassell & Biswas, 2000). On the other hand, it is also seen that the issue related with the problem of equality is a moral and social issue or just a commercial problem that needs management (Noon & Ogbonna, 2001). With relation to this, those who see equality as a problem of moral consequences usually support an approach of equality in opportunity (Kaler, 2001). Their view is based on the argument that no voluntary initiation has seen success while trying to find ways to eliminate discrimination. Thus, only an intervention of government through policies can bring equality and elimination of discrimination. This view of equality of opportunity tries to adopt the basic perspective of equality as well as discrimination (Liff, 1999), on the other hand, those who support the diversity management approach see these focus on equality as useless (Kandola & Fullerton,

8

1994a; Ross & Schneider, 1992). They instead focus on seeing the workers as people with special qualities in themselves that should be used in order to maximize business (Johnston & Packer, 1997).

Those studies that adopt the approach of diversity analyze both the scholarly merit as well as economic success that drives this method. Konrad (2003) has stated that scholarly reality of the topic of workplace diversity connected to the dynamics of power between small and big groups. She sees that the interest in the this topic has been due to the increase in power as well as representation of the groups that were usually neglected in the past. Interest in this topic has also been due to the idea that owning a workplace that is diverse may be a necessary and profitable aspect when trying to gain an advantage over others. Those who support this view believe that diverse workplace gives the organization the ability to understand as well as provide for various markets and give a variety in terms of workers that the organization can hire (Cox & Blake, 1991; Richard, 2000). Infact, some scholars have argued that when it comes to productivity of the organization, the diversity of the group often leads to better results (Robinson & Dechant, 1997).

Even though there is a wide interest in managing diverse workplace, there is lack of evidence in scholarly arguments. For instance, a major study by Kochan et al. (2003) failed to find any evidence associating gender as well as ethnic diversity with better performance in a positive way. It should be noted that some scholars have argued that instead of leading to creativity and productivity, a diverse workplace may indeed lead to inefficiency in an organization. Let us try to understand this. The social identity theory states that petiole label themselves as well as others on traits such as gender and race (Brunetto & Farr-Wharton, 2002). Thus, if a group is formed together of similar people, they might see it as a representation of their identity (Chattopadhyay et al., 2004; Tajfel & Turner, 1986). Those scholars who have worked in this approach have given a number of consequences related to performance in a workplace where diversity is the main factor (Hobman et al., 2003).

On the basis of this social identity theory, it's can explain why there is no evidence of a positive relation between diversity and performance. This was done in a research by Kochan et al. (2003). One do the findings is that the people of diverse groups often create distrust in others as well as a feeling of competition. They also show less affection to each other, which results in performance negatively (Harrison et al., 1998; Hogg et al., 1993). Additionally, it is also explored that this kind of difficulty that a diverse workplace faces is increased when communication is not fluent due to differences in language between minority and majority groups (Hambrick et al., 1998; Palich & Gomez-Mejia, 1999). On the basis of this we see that there are

9

certain perceptions of differences such as race, and then there are certain practical differences such as language. These two differences are highly likely to increase tension between two groups and lead to inability to function (Swann et al., 2004). In other words, this may lead to the organization not Huron people from diverse background into their workplace in order to avoid such conflicts and avoid the problems an organization might face in productivity. Many scholars have emphasized these problems (Dickens, 1999).

A lot of focus has been on the theme of disadvantages that minority groups feel. Scholars have researched this by seeing it in the light of disadvantages that minority groups feel in the process of hiring. A study that had imaginary applications for job from two people, one white and one black, it was seen that white person found more favors in terms of response (Noon, 1999).

Other scholars have studied this discrimination in relation to unemployment and come to the conclusion that people from minority groups were discriminated against by organizations more often that simply did not allow the minority group individual to get proper training to get work (Ogbonna, 1998).

Finally, it has been stated by many scholars that there is evidence to prove that while working, people from minority groups experience a great amount of difficulty when trying to get promotion (Jones, 1993).

A solution to this issue has to be taken with consideration to an understanding of how different relationship dynamics work between two groups.

6 References

Burkard, A., Boticki, M., & Madson, M. (2002). Workplace Discrimination, Prejudice, and Diversity Measurement: A Review of Instrumentation. *Journal of Career Assessment,* 343-361.

Fujimoto, Y. (2004). The Experience of Asian Expatriates in Australia. *Journal of Doing Business across Borders, 3*(1), 24-32.

Gandara, C. (2006). POST-9/11 Backlash Discrimination in the Workplace: Employers Beware of Potential Double Recovery. *Houston Business & Tax Law Journal, 7,* 169-200.

Grabowska, I., & Węziak-Białowolska, D. (2011). Discrimination at the Workplace – Findings from the European Working Condition Survey. Types of Discrimination Practices and their Characteristics. *Econometrics,* (31), 202-216.

Meares, M., Oetzel, J., Torres, A., Derkacs, D., & Ginossar, T. (n.d.). Employee Mistreatment and Muted Voices in the Culturally Diverse Workplace. *Journal of Applied Communication Research,* 4-27.

Ogbonna, E. (2006). The Dynamics of Employee Relationships in an Ethnically Diverse Workforce. *Human Relations,* 379-407.